T0195949

Lord, thanks

Stana Snodgrass Chapman

Graphics by Robert Chapman

WestBow Press books may be ordered through booksellers or by contacting:

WestBow Press
A Division of Thomas Nelson & Zondervan
1663 Liberty Drive
Bloomington, IN 47403
www.westbowpress.com
844-714-3454

Because of the dynamic nature of the Internet, any web addresses or links contained in this book may have changed since publication and may no longer be valid. The views expressed in this work are solely those of the author and do not necessarily reflect the views of the publisher, and the publisher hereby disclaims any responsibility for them.

Any people depicted in stock imagery provided by Getty Images are models, and such images are being used for illustrative purposes only.
Certain stock imagery © Getty Images.

ISBN: 978-1-6642-4486-3 (sc)
ISBN: 978-1-6642-4488-7 (hc)
ISBN: 978-1-6642-4487-0 (e)

Library of Congress Control Number: 2021918876

Print information available on the last page.

WestBow Press rev. date: 12/23/2021

WESTBOW
PRESS®
A DIVISION OF THOMAS NELSON
& ZONDERVAN

Thank you Lord for angels above
Thank you for my parents love.

Thank you Lord
For things that are funny
Thank you Lord for a cuddly bunny.

Thank Lord for Mom and Dad
Thank you Lord for hugs when I'm sad.

Thank you Lord
For the big green trees
Thank you Lord for the autumn leaves.

Thank you Lord for the mountains high
They look like they touch the sky.

Thank you Lord for flowers that bloom
Thank you Lord for naps at noon.

Thank you Lord for Bible school
Thank you Lord for the golden rule.

Thank you Lord for the food we eat
Thank you Lord for the friends we meet.

Thank you Lord for the summer bright
Nice long days with extra light.

Thank you Lord for the big blue sky
Thank you Lord for the planes that fly.

Thank you Lord for Grandma Dear
Thank you Lord for music I hear.

Thank you Lord for times at Church
Thank you Lord for Jesus First.

Thank you Lord for the ocean blue
Thank you Lord for the seagulls too.

Thank you Lord for my little sister.
When she's not here I always miss her.

Thank you Lord for the big oak trees
Thank you Lord for the birds and bees.

Thank you Lord for my birthday song
I will sing it all day long.

(COLOR HERE)

(COLOR HERE)

(COLOR HERE)

Printed in the United States
by Baker & Taylor Publisher Services